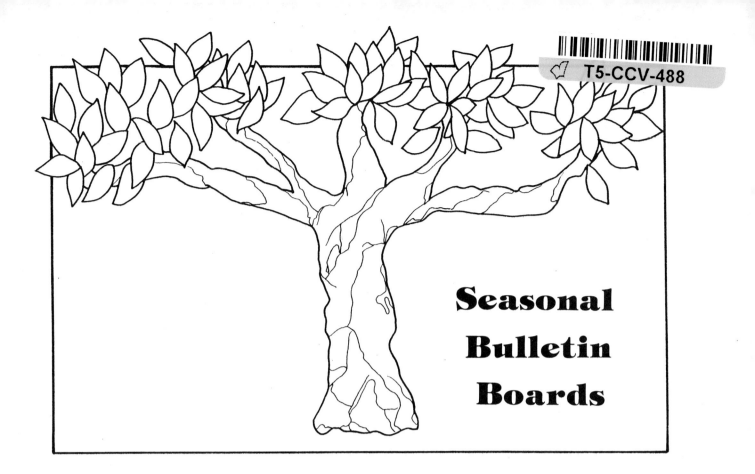

Seasonal Bulletin Boards

Contents

September

A board that changes...

Fall Fun

An activity board...

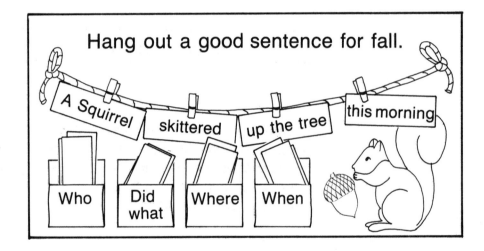

Hang out a good sentence for fall.

A Squirrel · skittered · up the tree · this morning

Who · Did what · Where · When

Over the chalkboard...

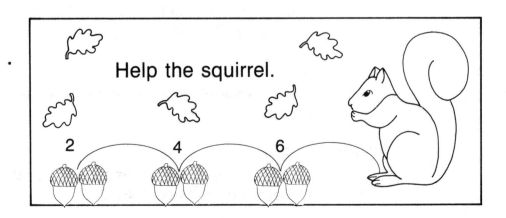

Help the squirrel.

2   4   6

Fall Fun

How to make:

Trunk

Crumble and twist brown paper bags. Pin these bags to the bulletin board in a tree shape. Allow the branches to bend and twist. Make the tree as large as your board permits. Why not let it extend over the top of the board?

Leaves

Pick a leaf shape from page 10. Cut green and orange leaves from the same pattern. Glue the leaves together. Pin the leaves to the tree with the green side showing.

Squirrel

Make a squirrel to climb the tree. Use the pattern on page 8.

Variations

Add acorns or apples to the tree branches. You will find acorn patterns on page 9.

How can this bulletin board change?

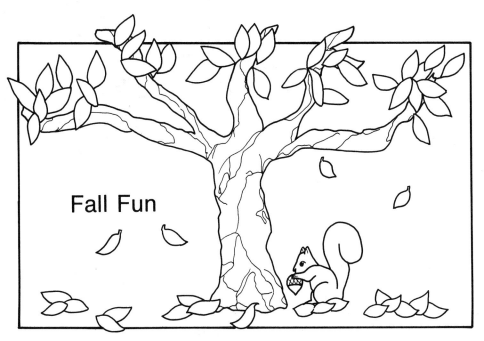

Leaves

Turn a few leaves over from green to orange each day. Begin to move the orange leaves from the branches to pile up below the tree. By the end of the month the tree's branches should be bare.

- Write a student's name on the orange side of each leaf. When the leaf falls from the tree, the child whose name appears on that leaf becomes student of the day.

- Write facts about fall on each orange leaf. Read and discuss each fact as the leaves fall.

- Put one fall writing topic on each leaf. As the leaves fall have your students write paragraphs, poems, or stories about the topic.

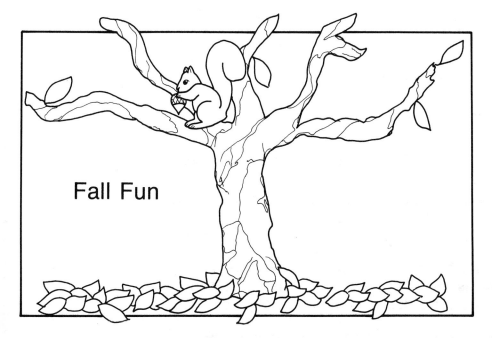

Acorns

Tuck a different acorn in the squirrel's paw each day. Ask the class a word problem (or have one written on each nut) about squirrels and the nuts they have collected for winter. Have the answers written on the back of the acorns.

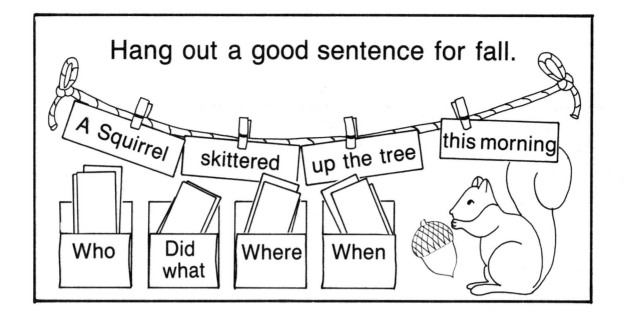

Hang out a good sentence for fall.

A Squirrel | skittered | up the tree | this morning

Who | Did what | Where | When

How to make:

Secure a line of rope across your bulletin board. Set it low enough for students to reach and change the tag strips hanging on the line. Hold the tag strips in place with clothespins.

Staple folders at the bottom of the board. You will need one folder for each category.

Cut tag strips to place in the folders.

Reproduce the squirrel pattern on page 8 and the acorn pattern on page 9. Pin them in the corner.

How to use:

Use language time to develop a whole set of fall sentence cards with your class. Write the words and phrases on the tag strips with felt pen.

Have children select cards from each category and arrange them into a sentence that makes sense. This board becomes a fine free time center for students to use throughout the season.

When	Where	Did What	Who
late at night.	under the fence	scampered	A squirrel
at 12:00.	over the moon	hid	That scarecrow
in September.	into a hole	disappeared	One pumpkin
last year.	behind the barn	darted	A little cat
just now.	on the doorstep	smiled	The mouse
		nibbled	Black bats

Over the chalkboard...

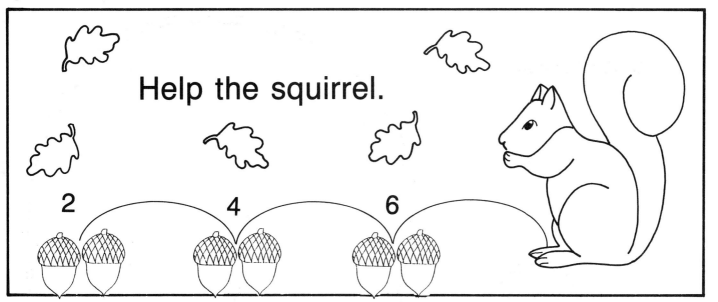

How to make:

Paint the "hop" marks with black paint on butcher paper or shelf paper.

Add a number or word at the end of each segment.

Reproduce the squirrel pattern on page 8.

Add leaves drifting down. Use the pattern on page 10.

Make acorns using the patterns on page 9.

How to use:

Use this board to practice information that comes in a particular sequence.

Counting by 2s, 5s, 10s 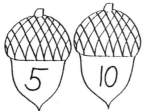   Roman Numerals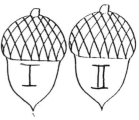

Days of the week 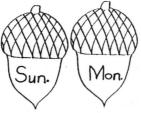   Months of the year

• Children can recite the sequence.

• Teacher can say a number or word, and the students can tell what comes before or after.

Squirrel Pattern

Seasonal Bulletin Boards

Acorn Patterns

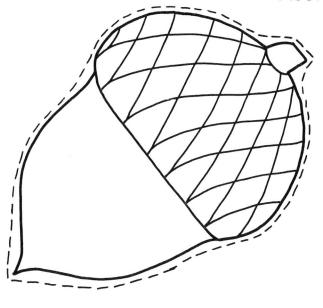 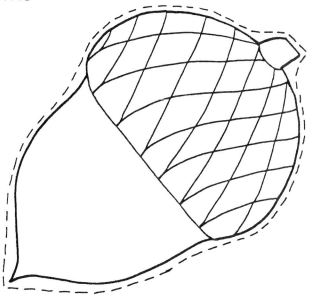

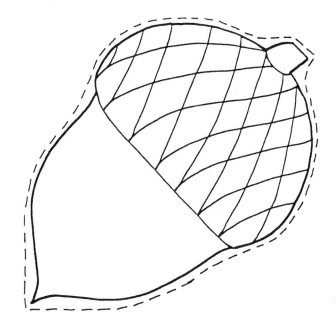 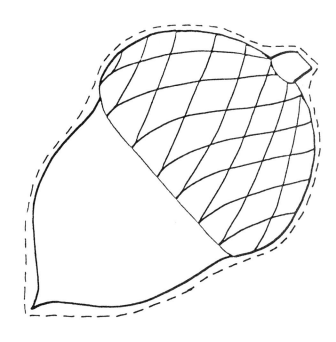

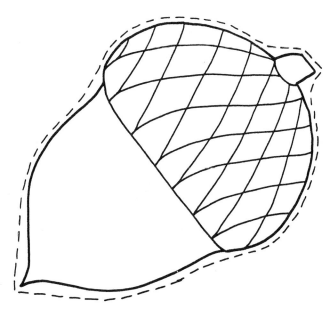 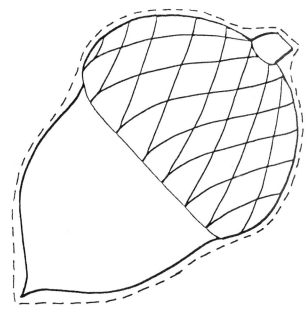

Fall Leaf Patterns

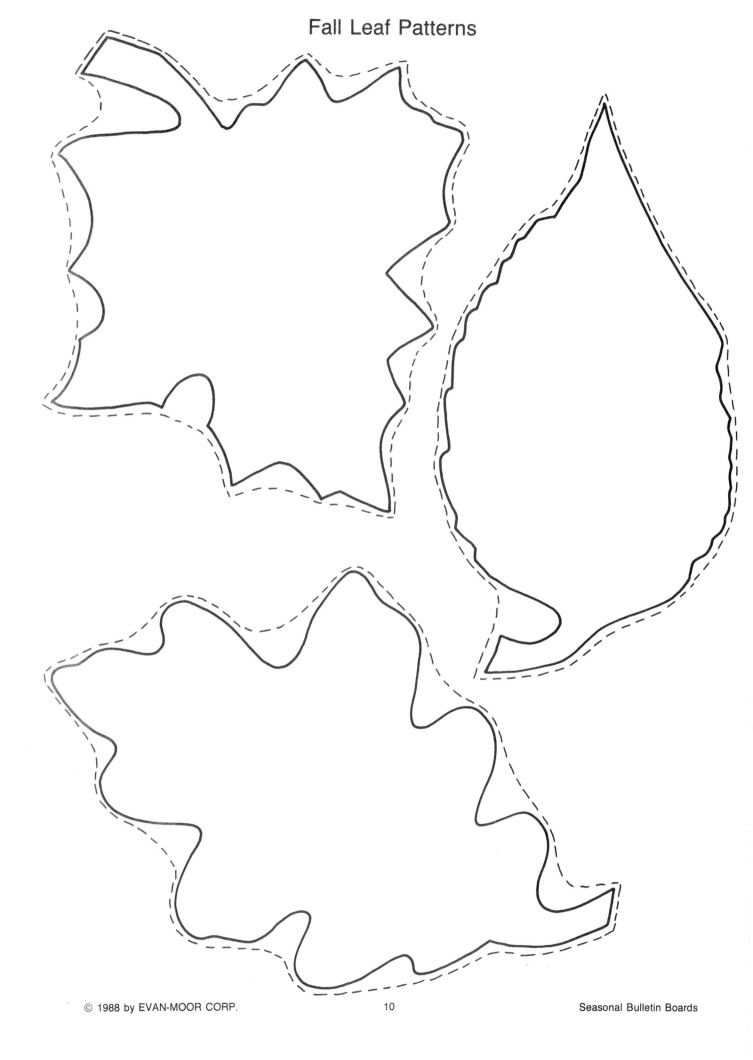

10   Seasonal Bulletin Boards

October

A board that changes...

Halloween Capers

An activity board...

A pumpkin grows.

The pumpkin seed sprouted.

Over the chalkboard...

Night Flight

bat

cat

sat

| How to make: |

Background

Cover the top 3/4 of the board with black butcher paper to make a night sky. Use green butcher paper to make a hill covering the bottom portion of the board. Make a full moon by cutting a circle out of white construction paper. (You may change the moon as the month passes.)

House

Use construction paper to create the house. Use whole rectangular sheets of dark blue paper to make the house. Cut a triangular shape for the roof out of brown paper. Use yellow paper cut in squares or rectangles for the windows. Add a brown door and a red chimney. Use black marker to draw window panes, a knob on the door, and bricks on the chimney. Add a walkway or stepping stones cut from brown or gray paper.

Make the porch from a brown triangle supported by straws.

How can this bulletin board change?

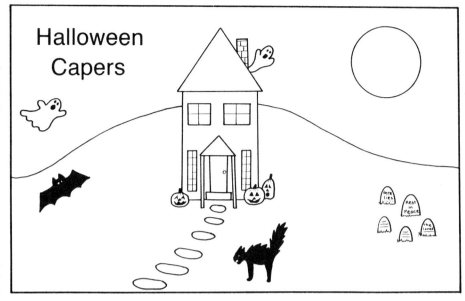

Each day add something to haunt the house. This can be done before school by the teacher as a surprise for the students or a child can be picked each day to make something to add to the house.

Things to haunt the house:

Jack-o'-lanterns can be cut in various shapes from orange construction paper. Add faces with black felt pen.

Ghosts can be cut from white construction paper or made from white facial tissues. Draw faces with black felt pen.

Cut black bat shapes from black construction paper.

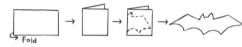

Make grave stones for the graveyard by rounding off the top of brown or grey construction paper rectangles.

Add things daily until Halloween. After school on Halloween, remove all of the "haunting" additions and put a few crumpled, empty candy wrappers on the lawn.

Teaching uses:

Discuss daily how the board has changed and what might appear tomorrow.

Predict how many ghosts or jack-o'-lanterns will appear.

Write a story about the house.

Count the number of bats, jack-o-lanterns, ghosts, etc.

If you change the moon, talk about each phase as it appears.

A pumpkin grows.

The pumpkin seed sprouted.

How to make:

Leaves
Use the pattern on page 16 to create leaves for the pumpkin plant.

Vines
Use 1'' wide strips of green construction paper. Twist them and pin loosely in place to form vines.

Blossom
Reproduce the pattern on page 16 to make a pumpkin blossom.

Pumpkins
Cut pumpkins in increasingly larger sizes. Cut the three smallest pumpkins from green construction paper. Cut the larger pumpkins from orange paper.

How to use:

The month begins with the pumpkin sprout just visible above the ground. Every couple of days add new leaves and vines. Next a small blossom shows, changing into a small green pumpkin. Begin to periodically replace the pumpkin on the bulletin board with a larger one. It is exciting to let the pumpkin grow into a huge orange ball. Right before Halloween paint a funny face on the pumpkin to create a giant jack-o-lantern. After Halloween start to crumble the pumpkin as though it was beginning to rot. Discuss this part of nature's cycle with your students.

Keep a class journal listing the growth and changes of the pumpkin plant. Each time a change occurs, write a sentence on a tag strip, and tape it on the side of the bulletin board. By the time the pumpkin is grown, you will have written the pumpkin's life cycle.

Over the chalkboard...

Night Flight

How to make:

Background
Cover the board with blue butcher paper.

Bats
Reproduce the bat pattern on page 19. Make as many as your board permits. You can also let the bats fly above the bulletin board.

Clouds
Cut free-form cloud shapes from white construction paper.

Moon
Cut a moon from bright yellow construction paper.

How to use:

Let your students come up with a list of "bat" rhyming words to write on the bat shapes.

Write bat couplets using the rhyming words. (Remind your students that a couplet is two lines that rhyme.)

You can use the same bat pattern to create a class shape book to hold these original bat couplets.

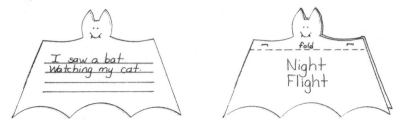

Pumpkin Leaf

Sprout

Blossom

Seasonal Bulletin Boards

Witch and Black Cat Patterns

Cut the witch and the cat from black paper on solid lines to make them silhouettes for the bulletin board. Dotted lines are provided for children if you want to use this as a color and cut page.

 Seasonal Bulletin Boards

Skeleton Pattern

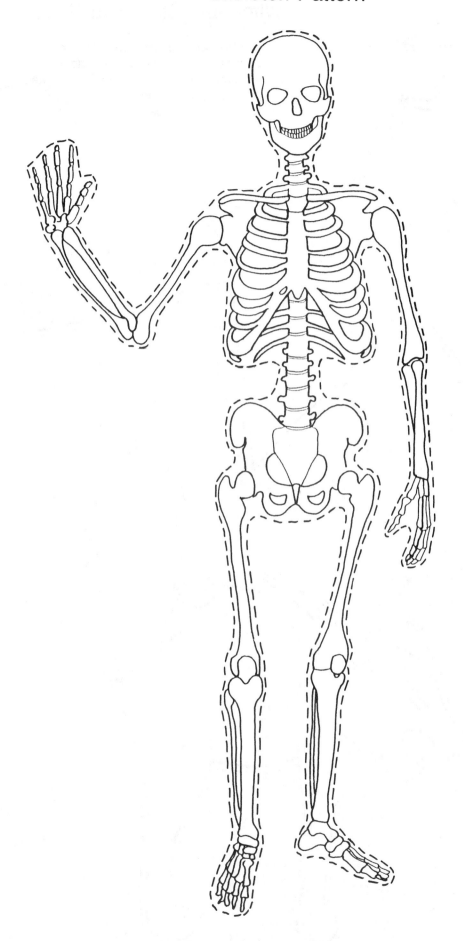

18

Seasonal Bulletin Boards

Bat Pattern

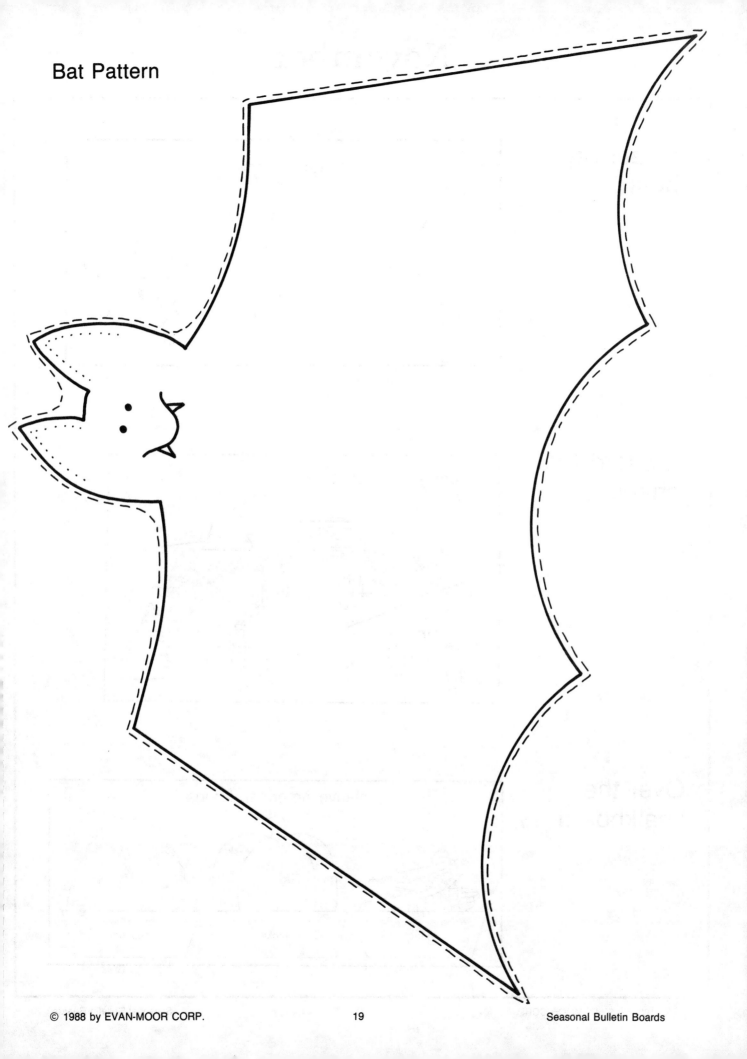

19

November

An activity board . . .

A board that changes . . .

Over the chalkboard . . .

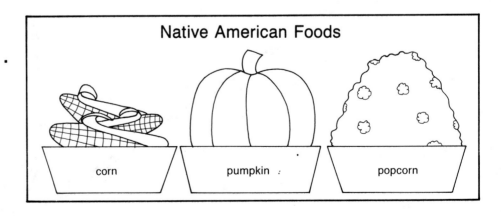

Seasonal Bulletin Boards

Turkey Talk

How to make:

These turkeys can be a valuable teaching tool for reinforcing patterning or counting skills.

Cut turkey parts from construction paper.

Add details with felt pen.

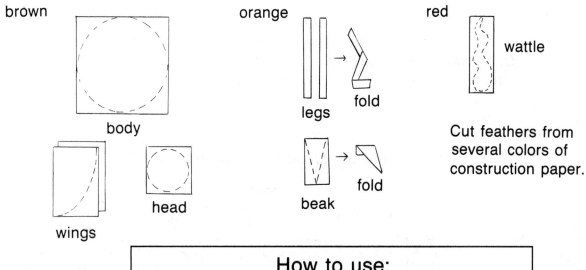

brown

body

wings

head

orange

legs

fold

beak

fold

red

wattle

Cut feathers from several colors of construction paper.

How to use:

1. Copy patterns

2. Count feathers

3. Practice word families

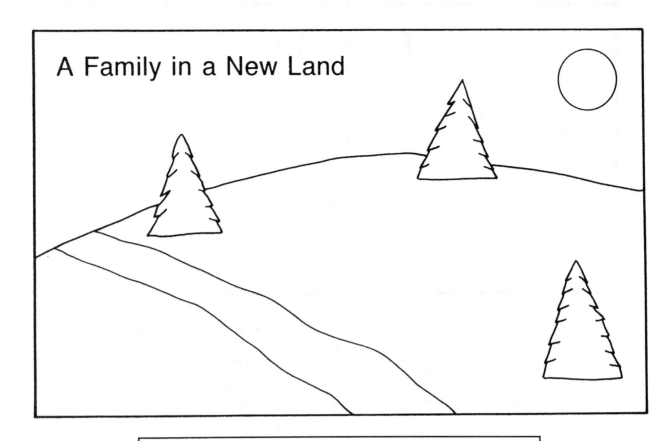

A Family in a New Land

How to make:

Background

Cover the bulletin board with light blue butcher paper. Cut brown butcher paper to form a hill. Cut a narrow strip of dark blue paper to create a river.

Trees

Cut the trees from folded green construction paper.

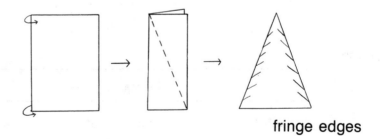

fringe edges

Sun

Cut a yellow sun from construction paper.

Discuss what wildlife existed in the new world at the time the Pilgrims arrived. Children may want to add animals such as deer, turkeys, squirrels, etc.

How can this bulletin board change?

A Family in a New Land

Students draw the pilgrim family in their work clothes and add them to the bulletin board. Discuss the types of work they might be doing to settle into their new home.

hunting   planting
cooking   chopping wood
baking   making candles
fishing

Now add the log cabin. Use the pattern on page 26.

A Family in a New Land

Perhaps the Indians are watching from behind a tree? Make the cabin from brown paper. Place a white sheet of paper underneath. Lift the brown "cabin" and draw some of the pilgrim family around the fire. Add a cooking pot over a fire in the yard.

Let students design and create the Thanksgiving feast table. Each student could draw himself/herself as a Pilgrim or Indian attending the feast.

This is a good time to introduce students to the nonfiction section of the library. Use these resources to collect information about early Pilgrim life. Intermediate students will enjoy gathering information about pioneer lifestyles and tools in the set of books by Edwin Tunis.

Over the chalkboard...

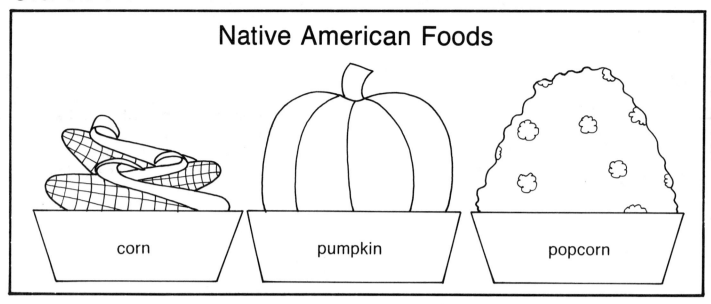

Native American Foods

corn   pumpkin   popcorn

How to make:

It is interesting to discuss what foods were native to this new land. You may cut the foods from construction paper or draw with felt tip pens. Cut brown construction paper "baskets" to hold each of the foods.

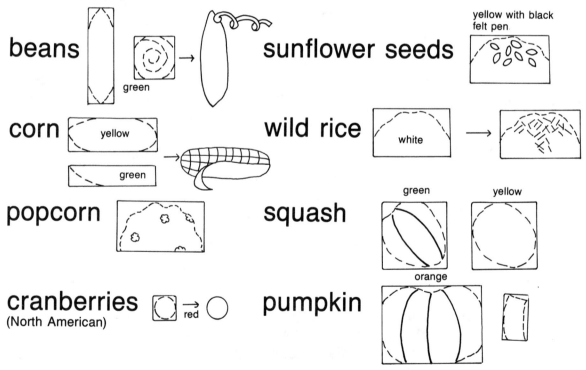

beans   green →

corn   yellow   green →

popcorn

cranberries
(North American)   → red

sunflower seeds   yellow with black felt pen

wild rice   white →

squash   green   yellow   orange

pumpkin

You may also want to point out the foods that traveled from South America to Europe and Africa, and then back to the U.S.A.

peppers   white potato   tomatoes
vanilla   sweet potato   pineapple
avocado   peanuts   chocolate

Also consider using The Mayflower Time Line produced by Evan-Moor Corp. It follows the Pilgrims on their trip across the Atlantic and develops facts about the journey.

24

How to Draw Indians and Pilgrims

Indians

Pilgrims

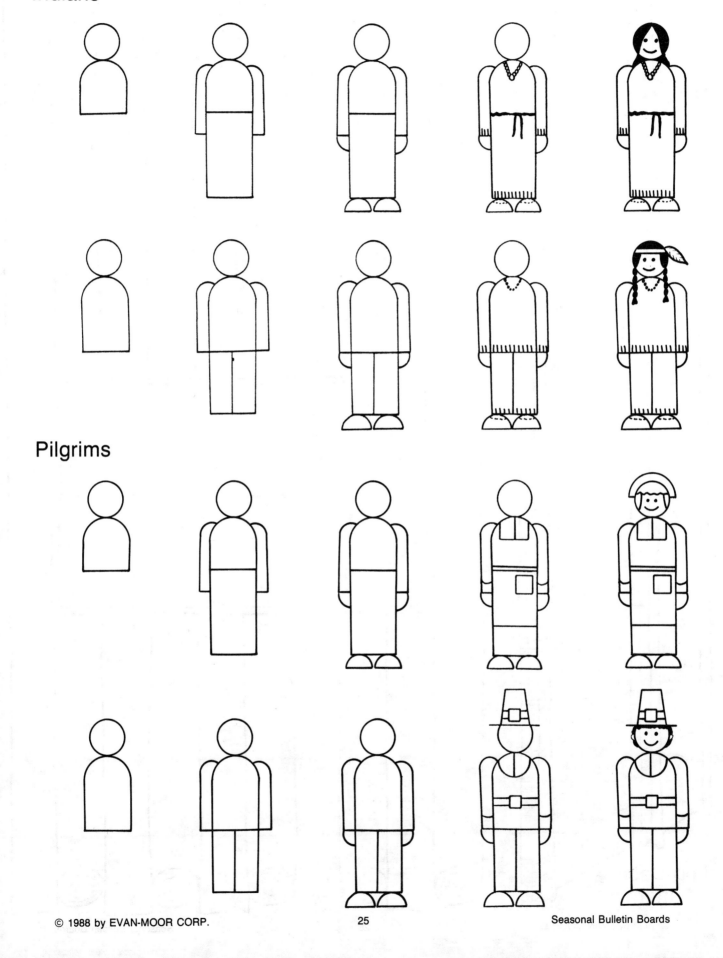

Log Cabin
Pattern

26   Seasonal Bulletin Boards

Name_____

Gobble! Gobble!

December

An activity board...

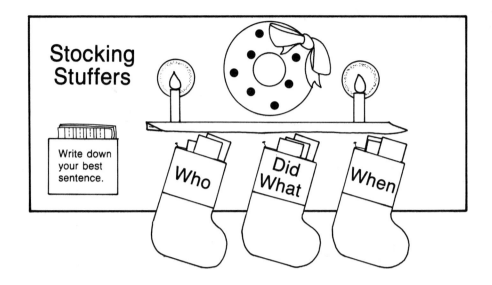

Stocking Stuffers

Write down your best sentence.

Who | Did What | When

A board that changes...

Sing hey! Sing hey!
For Christmas Day;
Twine mistletoe and holly,
For friendship glows
In winter snows,
And so let's all
be jolly!

unknown

Countdown
to
Christmas

Over the chalkboard...

On Dasher, on Dancer, on Prancer and Vixen...

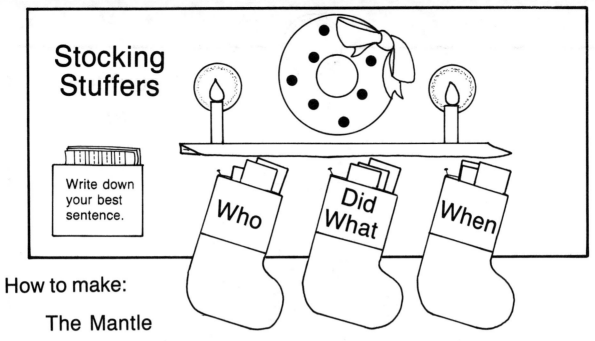

Stocking Stuffers

Write down your best sentence.

Who

Did What

When

How to make:

The Mantle

Fold brown construction paper and staple the lower section to the bulletin board. Let the top stick out.

Cut out candles and a wreath from construction paper.

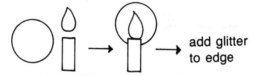 add glitter to edge

 add a bow and red berries

Stockings

Make 3 stockings from red felt. Glue or sew the front and back together. Glue a white pellon cuff just to the front section. Print the words Who, Did What, and When with a black felt pen.

Pin the stockings below the mantle. (You may want to add two more stockings for Where and Why.)

Phrase Cards

Cut tag sentence strips in half or thirds. Write appropriate phrases on the cards with black felt markers. Here are some suggestions to get you started.

Who	Did What	When
Three reindeer	practiced flying	before Santa left
Santa	slid down my chimney	in the middle of the night
Little elves	spilled paint	all winter
Mrs. Claus	fed the reindeer	while Santa rested
My dad	bought a tree	on December 16

Put the phrase cards in the correct stockings.

How to use:

Children select one card from each pocket and arrange the cards into a sentence. These can be sentences that make sense, or they can be silly sentences. You can have your students read the sentences they make orally or have them written down. It is fun to illustrate the sentences, especially the silly ones.

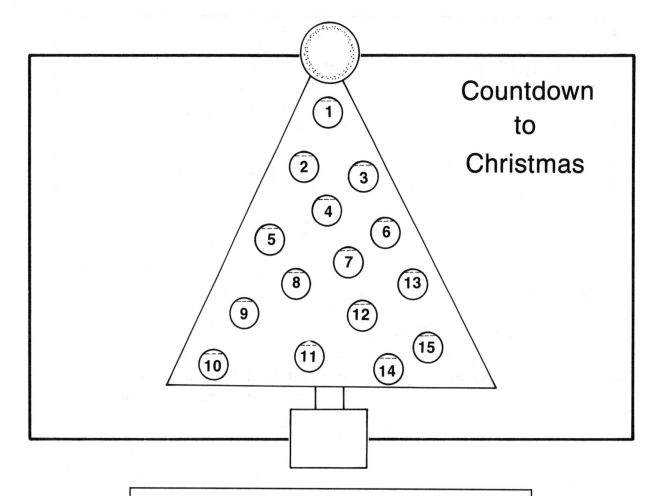

Countdown to Christmas

How to make:

The Tree

Cut the tree from a large sheet of green butcher paper. Cut it on the fold so that the tree is symmetrical.

Use a piece of brown construction paper for a trunk.

Attach a yellow square as a base for the tree.

 Cut a large yellow circle for the top of the tree. Add glitter to the edge for extra sparkle.

Ornaments

Cut a round, red ornament for each school day in December. Make numbers on the balls using white glue and glitter. Cut a white circle for each red ball. Glue the white circle behind the red ball at the top edge.

Write a surprise message, riddle, or Christmas wish on each white ball. Lower the red ball and tape shut at the bottom to prevent students from peeking.

Pin the ornaments to the tree. Mix up the numbers.

       Seasonal Bulletin Boards

How can this bulletin board change?

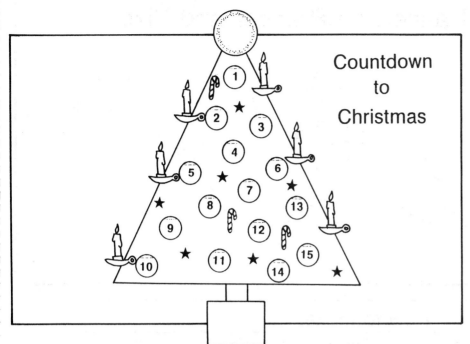

Countdown to Christmas

Each school day in December, select a different student to open the next ornament (open in numerical order), break the tape seal, and read the message inside. The surprise message could be a reward for the whole class or a Christmas riddle to share.

Sing hey! Sing hey!
For Christmas Day;
Twine mistletoe and holly,
For friendship glows
In winter snows,
And so let's all
be jolly!

unknown

Countdown to Christmas

Periodically during the month you may want to leave other surprises around your tree. (See the patterns on page 33.)

- a mouse peeking around the corner of the base
- candles on the tree
- a candy cane
- a teddy bear with a student's name on it for special recognition
- star stickers
- a Christmas poem

What surprises might you offer inside the ornaments?

- free reading time
- 5 minutes early to lunch
- a special art lesson
- an extra recess
- center time

- riddles

Why does Rudolph need an umbrella?
(He's a reindeer.)

Where do gingerbread men sleep?
(Under cookie sheets.)

Over the chalkboard...

On Dasher, on Dancer, on Prancer and Vixen...

How to make:

Use the reindeer pattern on page 34. Reproduce one reindeer for each student in class. Use a wide line black marker to put a number on each reindeer. Let each student color and cut out these reindeer. Pin them to your bulletin board in a long line.

How to use:

Each day spend five minutes using the reindeer to reinforce greater-than and less-than concepts.

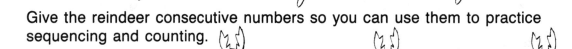

Give the reindeer consecutive numbers so you can use them to practice sequencing and counting.

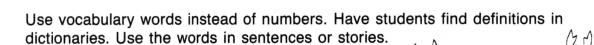

Use vocabulary words instead of numbers. Have students find definitions in dictionaries. Use the words in sentences or stories.

33

Reindeer Pattern

 Seasonal Bulletin Boards

January

A board that changes...

An activity board...

Over the chalkboard...

A Blizzard of New Year Wishes

How to make:

Background

Back the bulletin board with blue butcher paper.

Snowflakes

1. Fold a square piece of paper.
(Use a light weight paper.)

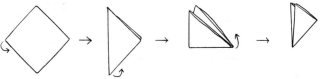

2. Create your own design by cutting away as much as you desire. Open the finished snowflake and check the design. You may need to refold and cut away more paper to achieve a snowflake you like.

3. Scatter the snowflakes across the bulletin board. Pin them in place.

This can become a writing activity using the circle forms on page 40. Have your students write about winter (poem, paragraph, descriptive sentence) on the forms, cut them out, and paste their circles into the middle of their snowflakes.

How can this bulletin board change?

A Blizzard of New Year Wishes

Gradually rearrange the snowflakes so that they have all fallen to the bottom of the board creating a snowdrift.

After a day or so, begin to build a snowman. Cut the basic shapes from paper.

Each day add something new to the snowman until he is complete.

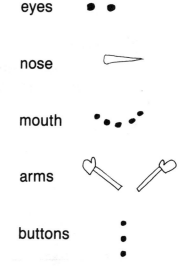

eyes

nose

mouth

arms

buttons

A Blizzard of New Year Wishes

Top him off with a hat out of someone's closet, or try the lost and found.

Other suggestions:

Post a copy of your favorite snow poem beside the snowman.

Have children write adventures for the snowman. Display these original stories by the snowman.

   Seasonal Bulletin Boards

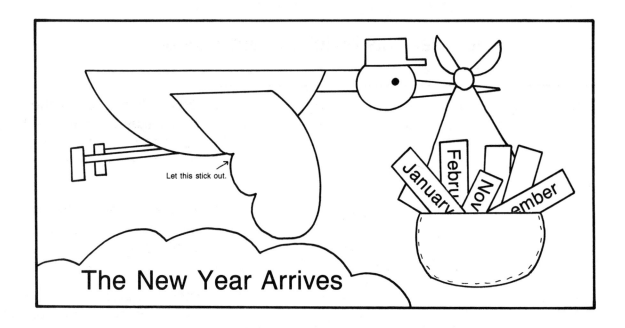

The New Year Arrives

How to make:

Background

Cover the bulletin board with blue butcher paper. Cut a white cloud shape to put on the lower edge.

Stork

white

body

wing

neck

head

orange

feet

beak

red

cap

yellow

bundle

Staple this piece to the bundle.

How to use:

Print the names of the months on tag strips. Children can remove the strips and play "Put the Months in Order." Put a small number on the back of each month so that this activity can be self-checking.

Other activities:

Teach your class the poem 30 Days Hath September.

Use *Anno's Counting Book* to develop a unit on the months and seasons.

Tracks In the Snow

How to make:

Cover your bulletin board with white paper. Create animal tracks across the board. These may be cut from black construction paper and pinned to the board or painted directly on the white paper with black tempera. You can use this board to introduce students to using an encyclopedia to find information. If you look up TRACKS, you will discover a wonderful resource section on the shape of various animal tracks. *Big Tracks, Little Tracks* by Franklyn M. Branley (Scholastic Book Services) is a good source if you are working with young students.

RABBIT   DOG   CAT   ROBIN

Cut a red question mark from construction paper to place at the end of each track. Print a number on the dot of the question mark to identify the set of tracks. On the back of the dot, write the name of the animal that makes the tracks.

How to use:

1. Let students guess who owns the tracks. Take a class tally.
2. Discuss how to find information about animal tracks in the library. Use the encyclopedia or other reference books to collect the information. Check what they find out about tracks against the tally of guesses your students made.
3. Write stories about the animals who made the tracks and how they survive the winter.

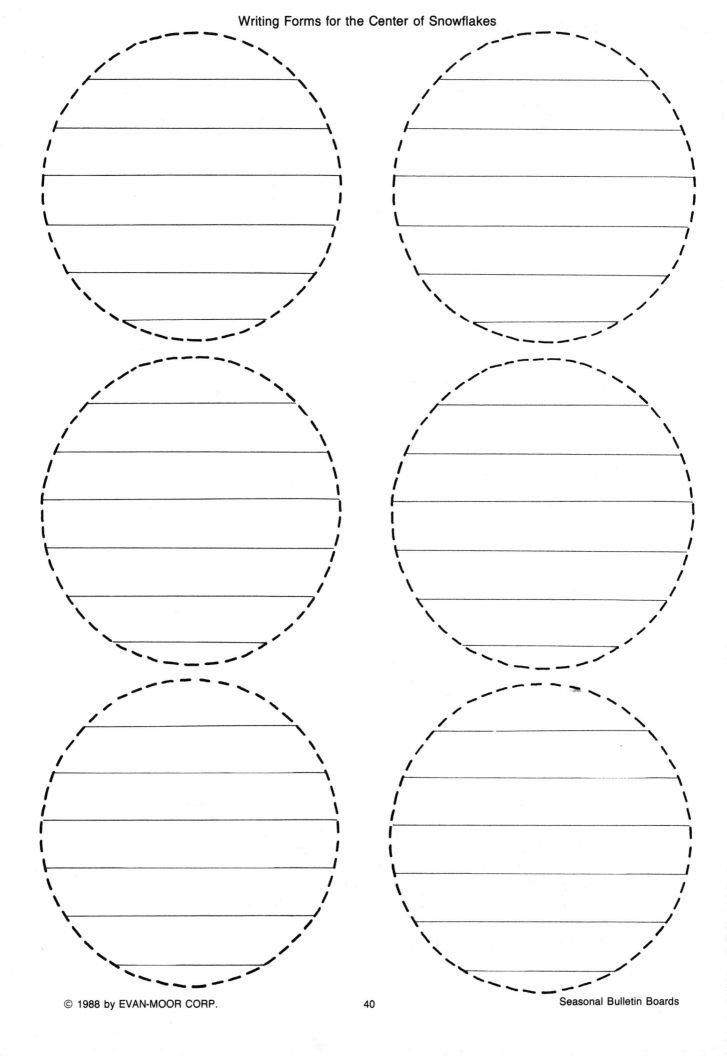

40

February

A board that
changes...

Aim at being
a good friend!

An activity
board...

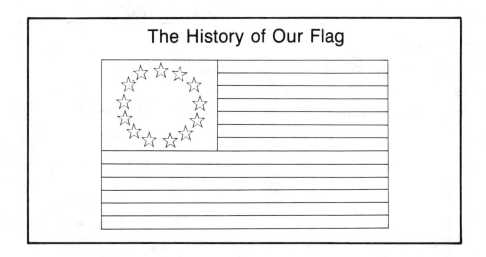

The History of Our Flag

Over the
chalkboard...

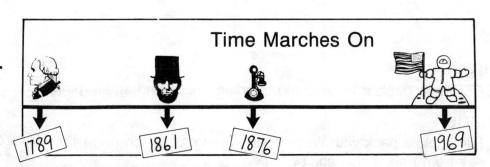

Time Marches On

1789   1861   1876   1969

Aim at being
a good friend!

How to make:

Background

Cover the bulletin board with blue butcher paper.

Cut a white cloud shape for the lower edge.

Paint the caption with black tempera directly on the cloud.

Cut hair from black construction paper.

Cupid

red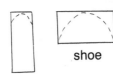

body
arm
shoe

white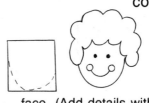

wing
face (Add details with felt pen.)

hand

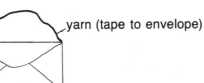

yarn (tape to envelope)

envelope

Bow

black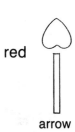

yarn

red

arrow

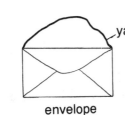

Target

Cut three circles: large (pink), medium (red), and small (pink)

Hearts

Fill Cupid's pack with these hearts (see pattern on page 47). Make one heart for each school day from Feb. 1 to Feb. 14.

Staple two hearts together at the side.
Lift the top heart and write a good deed inside.
Tape the heart shut so no one can peek.

   Seasonal Bulletin Boards

How can this bulletin board change?

Each day let a student select one heart from Cupid's pack, break the seal, and read the good deed to be done that day. Pin that heart inside the target for the day.

Each afternoon give student's 5 to 10 minutes to write in a "Friendship Journal." Let them explain each day how they have fulfilled the good deed on the heart. (See heart writing form on page 48.) At this time, remove the current day's heart from the target and pin it to the bottom of the bulletin board.

Possible Good Deeds:

Compliment someone's work.

Hold the door open for a friend.

Help someone solve a problem.

Thank someone at school (custodian, librarian, nurse, etc.) for how they help make it a good school.

Clean up a mess, even if you didn't make it.

The History of Our Flag

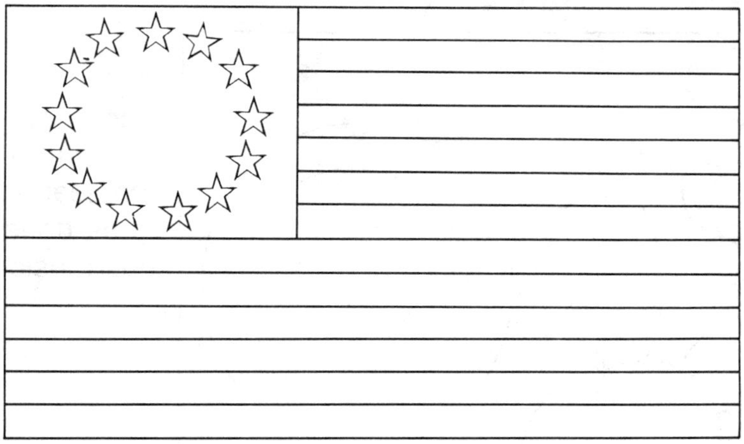

How to make:

Cover the bulletin board with white butcher paper. Outline the flag area with black yarn. Make the flag as large as possible. Cut blue construction paper for the star field. Cut long strips of red butcher paper for the 7 red strips. Pin them in place.

Reproduce the star pattern on page 47.

How to use:

Throughout this month, discuss the story of the development of the flag of the U.S.A. Begin with the original 13-star, and periodically switch the blue field and stars to show the changes.

Hint: Make separate fields so you can change the whole section each time.

Jan. 1, 1776 — The flag had seven red and six white alternating stripes and the British Grand Union flag in the canton. (This showed loyalty to the crown since the colonists weren't yet planning independence.)

June 14, 1777 — The Continental Congress adopted a design for the national flag. It was to have 13 stripes, alternating red and white, and 13 stars of white on a blue field. No rule was made at that time as to how the stars were to be arranged. Some flags had 13 stars in a circle, some had 12 stars in a circle with one in the center, and others had three rows of stars (4, 5, 4).

May 1, 1795 — Congress voted to add two stripes and two stars for the new states Vermont and Kentucky. The flag contained 15 stars and 15 stripes until 1818.

April 4, 1818 — Congress voted that the flag would have 13 stripes alternating red and white to represent the original 13 states, and a star for each state in the union. In 1818 the flag contained 20 stars.

July 4, 1960 — The flag reached its present appearance with 13 stripes of red and white, plus 50 stars arranged in nine rows alternating six and five stars.

Over the chalkboard...

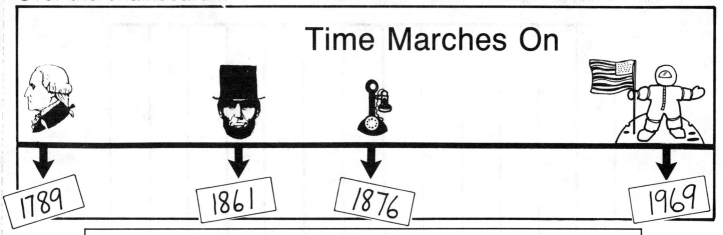

Time Marches On

1789   1861   1876   1969

How to make:

Time lines are valuable teaching tools. This one is easy to construct and provides an opportunity to open interesting class discussions.

Cover your bulletin board with butcher paper or shelf paper. Stretch a piece of roving across the board. Mark each date you wish to emphasize with an arrow. Label the date and the event it represents below the arrow. Add a picture from your picture file.

How to use:

This time line helps build the concept of the span of time that separates Washington, Lincoln, and modern times. This is also a chance to highlight other interesting events occurring during the time shown.

1789   George Washington becomes President
1792   Kentucky became the 15th state
1814   Star-Spangled Banner composed by Francis Scott Key
1837   Patent for the manufacture of rubber obtained by Charles Goodyear
1844   First telegraph message sent
1848   Gold discovered in California
1860   Pony Express service from Missouri to California started
1861   Abraham Lincoln becomes President
1862   Emancipation Proclamation
1864   Lee surrendered to Grant ending the Civil War
1876   Alexander Graham Bell transmitted the sound of a human voice over the telephone
1879   Edison invented the first electric lamp
1903   The Wright brothers flew their plane at Kitty Hawk, North Carolina
1941   Japan attacked Pearl Harbor
1945   United Nations charter signed in San Francisco, CA
1959   Alaska and Hawaii became the 49th and 50th states in the U.S.A.
1961   Peace Corps created
1962   John Glenn became the first American astronaut to be put in orbit
1963   200,000 Americans took part in a civil rights march in Washington, D.C.
1969   Astronauts Neil Armstrong and Edwin Aldrin landed on the moon
1976   Bicentennial of the U.S.A. (200 years since the Delcaration of Independence was signed)
1981

NOTE: Use this as a follow-up worksheet with the activity on page 44.

Flag Pattern

Stars and Heart

Seasonal Bulletin Boards

March

A board that
changes...

An activity
board...

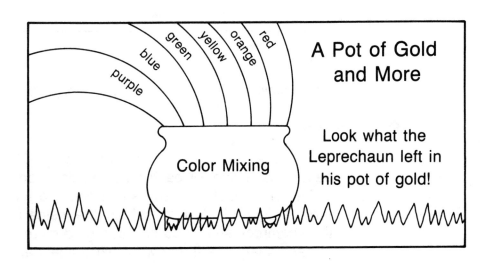

Over the
chalkboard...

It's Your Good Luck Day

What does this shamrock say?

How to make:

Background

Use yellow butcher paper for the background.

Shamrocks

Reproduce the shamrock pattern on page 55 on green paper. Make one for each teaching day from March 1 to March 17. Cut out each shamrock and fold to close. Write a "good luck surprise" on the inside flap. Tape the shamrock shut. You can add gold glitter to the edge of each shamrock if you want extra sparkle.

Mushroom

Make a large red mushroom from butcher paper. Add large white spots.

Enlarge pattern on page 57 if you want a guide.

Leprechaun

Reproduce the leprechaun pattern on page 54. Color, cut out, and pin him on top of the mushroom.

How can this bulletin board change?

Each day select a child to pick one shamrock. After the shamrock has been read, place it in the leprechaun's hand for the day. At the end of the day, place it along the edge of the bulletin board. As the days pass, a shamrock border will begin to form around the board.

Suggestions for Good Luck Surprises:

- 5 minutes more at recess
- Teacher will read to the class an extra 10 minutes from a book they choose.
- Art time today! (Have a lesson ready!)
- A special snack
- Video after lunch
- An indoor game

       Seasonal Bulletin Boards

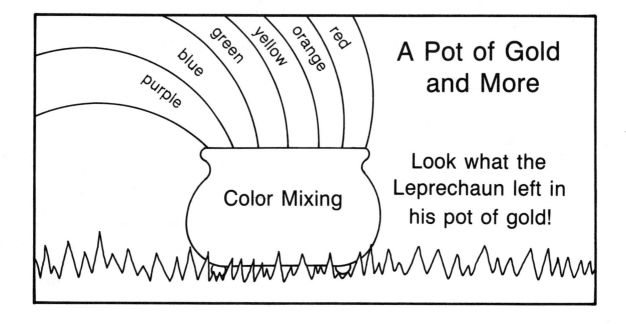

A Pot of Gold and More

Look what the Leprechaun left in his pot of gold!

How to make:

Background

Cover your bulletin board with white butcher paper. Sketch the rainbow lines in lightly with pencil. Begin by painting red, yellow, and blue.

Pot of Gold

Cut the pot from black butcher paper. Add circles for feet.

How to use:

Mix red, yellow, and blue food coloring with water in clear plastic glasses. (Large groups of children can enjoy this lesson if you set the glasses on an overhead projector as you mix colors.) Now mix new colors from the red, yellow, and blue.

1. Mix red and yellow to make orange.
2. Mix yellow and blue to make green.
3. Mix red and blue to make purple.

Select students to paint in the missing rainbow colors on the bulletin board.

Reproduce the color wheel on page 56 for your class. They can color in the appropriate circles as the color mixing lesson proceeds.

Give older students primary paint colors. Have them mix their own secondary colors.

Over the chalkboard...

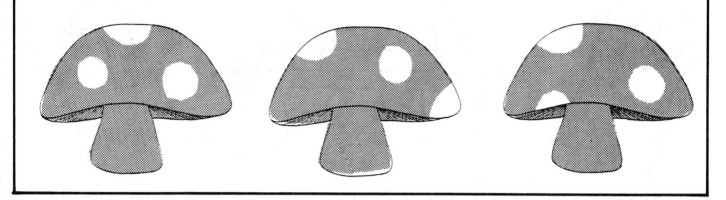

Mushroom Magic

How to make:

Cover the bulletin board with green or blue paper.

Reproduce the mushroom pattern on page 57 on red paper. Cut out white spots and paste them on the mushrooms.

How to use:

Use these mushrooms to reinforce several different skills.

- Positional Words — Cut a caterpillar from green construction paper. Place him in a different position each day; over, under, or beside a mushroom. Ask students to identify his placement.

- Ordinal numbers — Pin 10 mushrooms in a line. Reproduce the leprechaun pattern on page 54. Each day have the leprechaun perch on a different mushroom. Ask "Where is the leprechaun today?"

- Counting — Count the dots on each mushroom.

Sitting Leprechaun
Pattern

Shamrock Patterns

Seasonal Bulletin Boards

Name_____

My Color Wheel

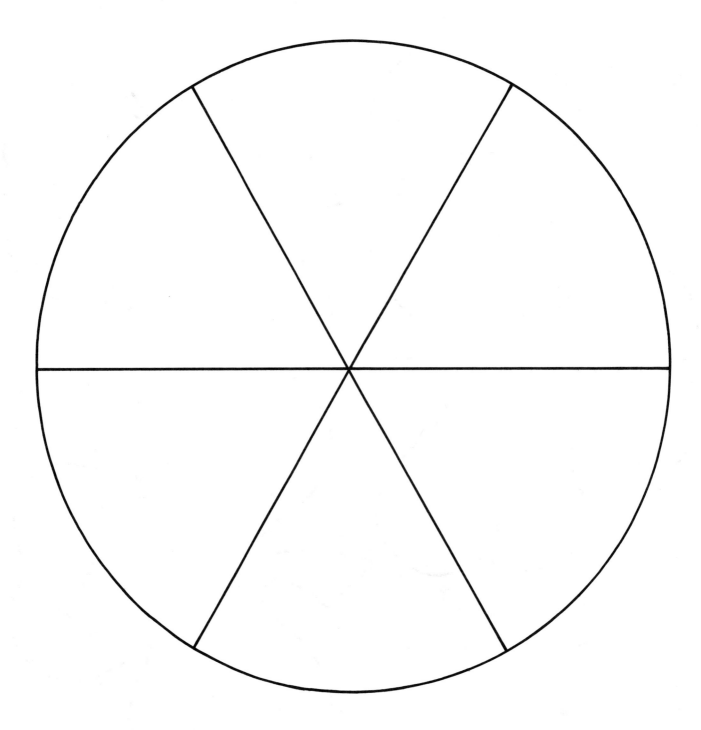

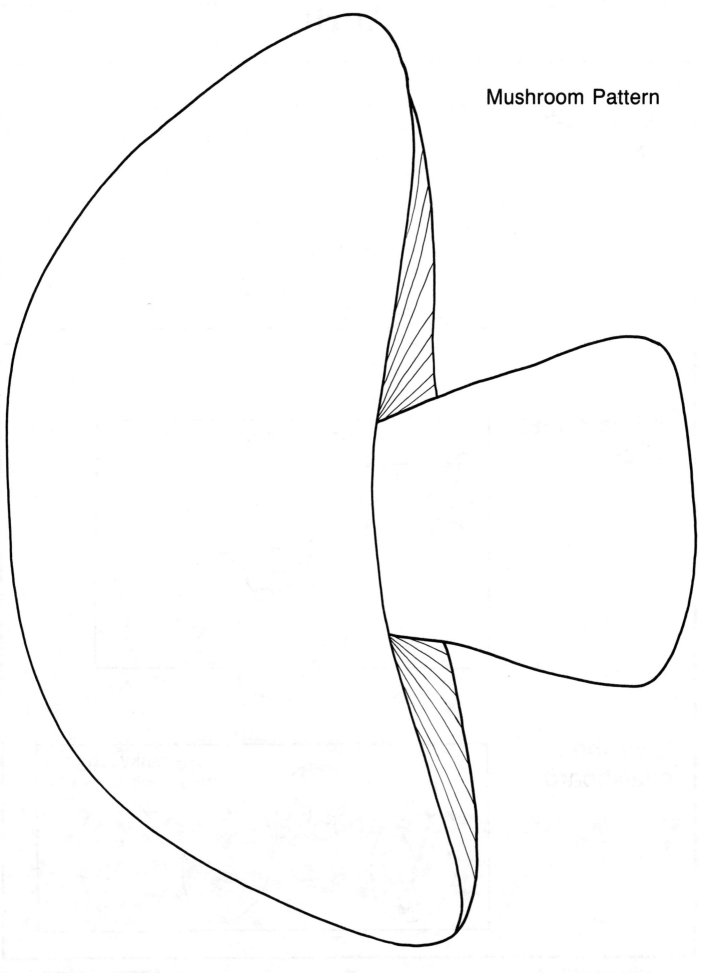

Mushroom Pattern

Seasonal Bulletin Boards

April

An activity board . . .

Bunny Business

Can you find 5 carrots for each pocket?

[5 five] [6 six]

[7 seven] [8 eight]

A board that changes . . .

April is full of surprises!

Over the chalkboard . . .

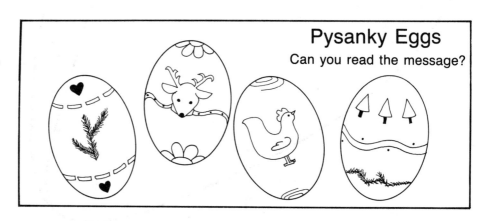

Pysanky Eggs
Can you read the message?

Bunny Business

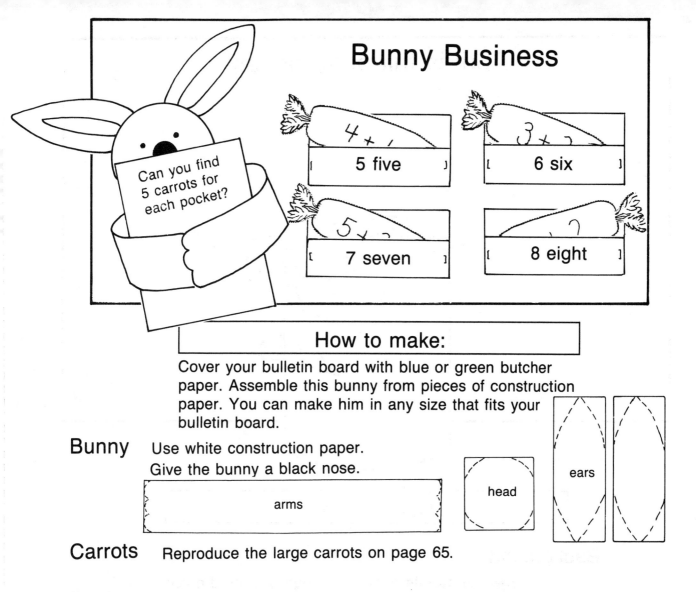

Can you find 5 carrots for each pocket?

4 + 1   5 five
3 + 3   6 six
5 + 2   7 seven
         8 eight

How to make:

Cover your bulletin board with blue or green butcher paper. Assemble this bunny from pieces of construction paper. You can make him in any size that fits your bulletin board.

Bunny Use white construction paper.
Give the bunny a black nose.

arms

head

ears

Carrots Reproduce the large carrots on page 65.

Pockets Make these pockets from brown wrapping paper. Staple the sides closed.

How to use:

This bunny can be used to reinforce many skills. All you have to do is change the carrots.

- Math Facts:
  Put a number word or numeral on each pocket front. Write math problems on each carrot. (Select a computation skill your group needs to practice.) Be sure you have five correct answers for each pocket. Pass the carrots out to your group. Each child must find the correct pocket for his/her answer.
- Categories:
  Write the name of the category on each pocket front. Write words or put pictures on each carrot. The carrots must be placed into the correct category pocket.
- Facts about _____:
  Place people or events from history on the pocket fronts (name or picture). Write facts about the person or event on the carrots. The carrots must then be placed in the correct pocket.

April is full of surprises!

How to make:

Background

Cover the bulletin board in a brightly colored butcher paper — pink, yellow, or blue.

Hat

Cut the hat from black construction paper.

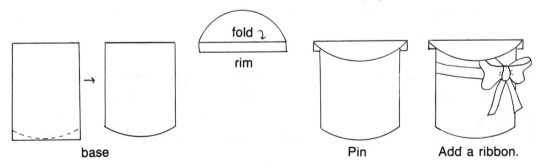

base   fold ↲   rim   Pin   Add a ribbon.

Bunnies

Reproduce the bunny pattern on page 63.
1. Enlarge it if you want it bigger.
2. Reproduce it in several different colors or all white.

How can this bulletin board change?

April is full of surprises!

Each day a new bunny is pulled from the hat and pinned to the board. (Tuck a bunny or two in the hat before class each day. Leave part of the ears sticking out to give something to pull.)

April is full of surprises!

Make the last bunny you pull out a surprise.

A different color or material
A bunny with freckles or measles
Not a bunny but something funny like a hippo

How can you use the bunnies?

- Put vocabulary words on the bunnies. At the end of each week (or the month) write sentences or stories using the words.
- Put words or phrases on the bunnies. At the end of the week unscramble the words to create a sentence about bunnies or Easter.
- Number the bunnies 1-30. Mix them up. Have your students put them in order on the last day of the month. (You may use word names, ordinal numbers, or Roman numerals to make it more challenging for older students.)
- Make pairs of bunnies identical by adding colorful touches such as bow ties, vests, etc. Have your students match each bunny with its pair at the end of the month.

Pysanky Eggs

Can you read the message?

How to make:

Ukrainian Easter eggs (Pysanky eggs) are decorated with symbols of good wishes. These beautiful eggs are given to special friends and family members.

Cut egg shapes out of construction paper.

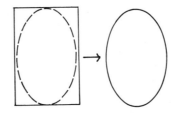

Let students sketch their message lightly with pencil. Then they may decorate the eggs with colorful designs using crayons, chalk or pastels, paint, or felt pens.

Here are some symbols and what they mean:

spiral — growing   flower — love   pine tree — love   reindeer — wealth

hen and rooster — wishes coming true

     Seasonal Bulletin Boards

Rabbit Patterns

Seasonal Bulletin Boards

Note: Use these small carrots to create worksheets for your students.

Bunny Lunch
Crunch! Crunch!

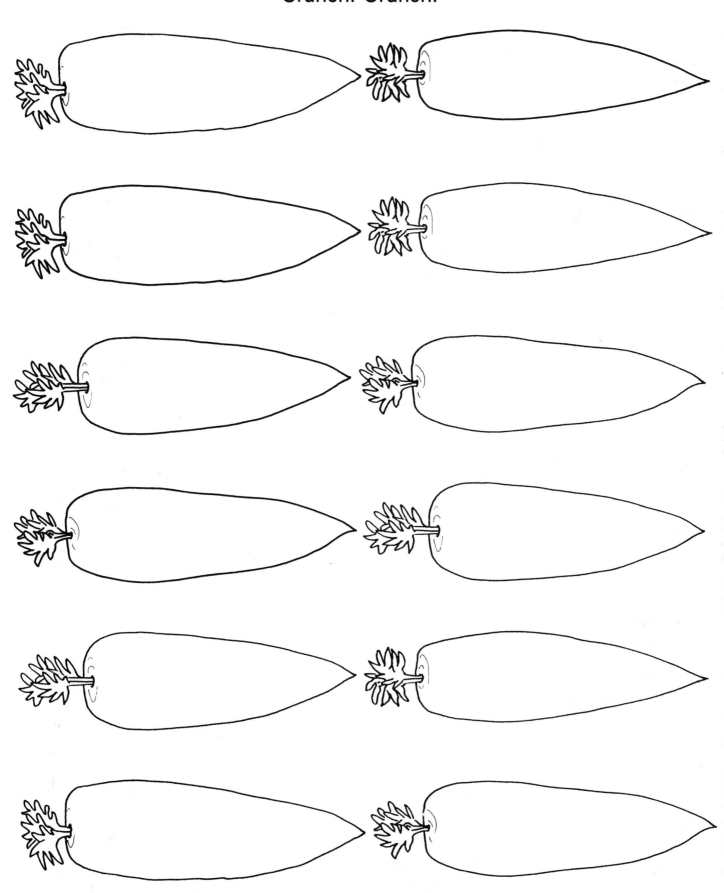

Carrot Patterns

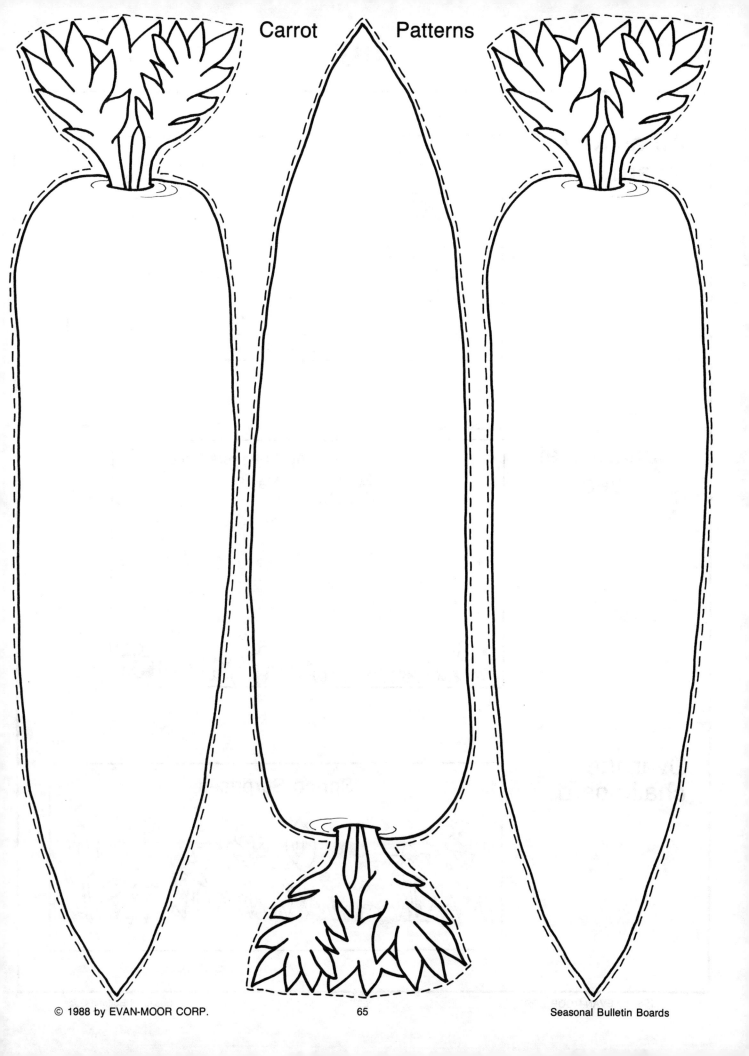

Seasonal Bulletin Boards

May

An activity board...

A board that changes...

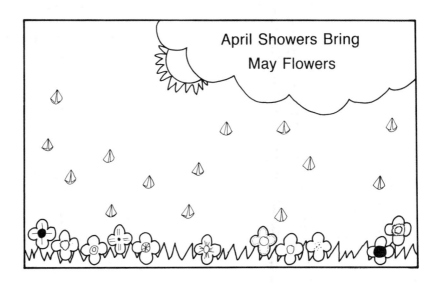

Over the chalkboard...

How to make:

This bulletin board provides an opportunity to highlight a different student's work each day. The class, as a whole, completes a writing lesson about their moms. They also create pictures of their moms (head only) on 9" X 12" sheets of art paper.

Background

Cover the bulletin board with any color of butcher paper.

Figures

Cut the body parts from construction paper.

shoulders:

collar

buttons

stripes

child's head:

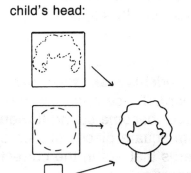

speech bubble:
Cut from white construction paper.
Add a paper clip.

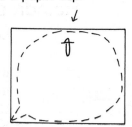

How to use:

Each day pin a different picture on mom's shoulders. Pin the accompanying story in the speech bubble.

Students do not sign their works. The rest of the class tries to guess each day who the mystery mom might be.

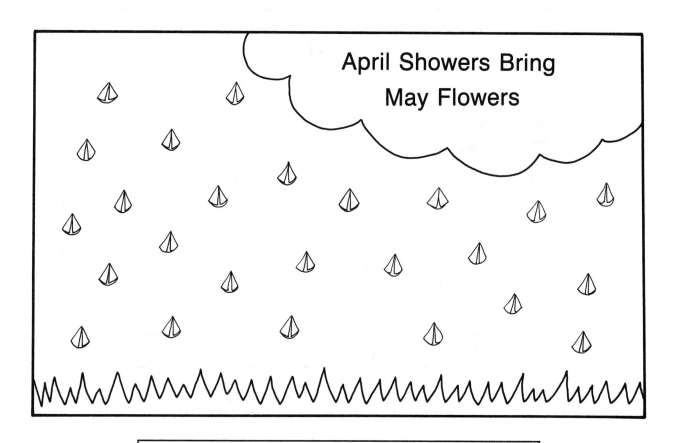

April Showers Bring
May Flowers

How to make:

Background

Cover the bulletin board in light blue construction paper.

Cut a green grass border to go along the bottom.

Cut a cloud from white butcher paper for the top of the board. Paint on the caption.

Raindrops

Let your students make their own raindrops to pin up on the board. These raindrops are appropriate because they actually *become* spring flowers. The raindrops are made from square pieces of blue construction paper. Use squares that are in the correct proportion for your bulletin board.

Fold the paper and trim off the tip.

Now for the surprise! Open the raindrop and create a colorful flower on the inside.

Fold the raindrops back up and pin them to the bulletin board.

How can this bulletin board change?

Periodically move a few raindrops down to the grass and open them up to show the flower inside.

Cut out a yellow sun to peek out from behind the cloud.

By the end of the month all the raindrops should have landed in the grass and blossomed into a flower. The sun is now in full view.

You now have lots of bulletin board space to display children's spring stories and poems.

The raindrops are blessed
With showers of power.
They can coax a seed
Into a lovely flower.

Leslie Tryon

Puffy clouds and
dancing crowds
of wildflowers
on the hill.

A breeze comes along
and lifts a song
that chases away
winter's chill.

Leslie Tryon

Over the chalkboard...

Spring Surprises

How to make:

Background

Cover the board with light blue butcher paper.
Cut grass by fringing thin strips of green butcher paper.

Flowers

Materials needed: (all flowers are made from construction paper)

- Iris — reproduce the pattern on page 72 on bright blue paper
  one 1'' X 18'' green strip for the stem and leaf
  one 2'' X 6'' yellow strip for the stamen

- Daffodil — reproduce the pattern on page 74 on yellow paper
  one 1'' X 18'' green strip for the stem and leaf

- Calla lily — reproduce the pattern on page 73 on white paper
  one 1'' X 18'' green strip for the stem and leaf
  one 1'' X 6'' orange strip for the stamen

- Poppy — reproduce the pattern on page 74 on orange paper
  one 1/4'' X 6'' green strip for the stem

How to make:

Iris

Cut out the pattern.

Fringe one end of the yellow.

Paste the other end to the stem.

Put the stamen on the pattern, and fold the blue to make the flower.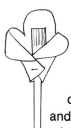

fold back

staple

Cut a point on the other end of the stem, and fold up to make the leaf.

Daffodil

Cut out both parts of the pattern.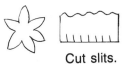

Cut slits.

Paste into a cylinder.

Fold the slits toward the center of the cylinder.

(It may be easier for younger children to fold the slits out.)

Paste the cylinder onto the middle of the flower. Paste on the stem.

Cut a point on the other end of the stem. Fold up to make the leaf.

Calla lily

Cut out the pattern.

Round off one end of the orange to make the stamen.

Use white and yellow crayons to color pollen on the stamen.

Paste the stem to the stamen, and lay it inside the flower pattern. Curl the edges around the stamen to form the flower.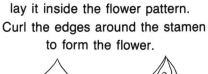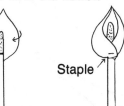

Staple

Cut a point on the other end of the stem, and fold up to make a leaf.

Poppy

Cut out the pattern and fold:

Open the flower up.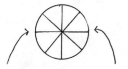

Pinch in the side folds.

Paste the stem on the flower.

How to use:

- Use these flowers to create a garden in your room. Teach the names of the flowers, compare them, and learn to recognize them.
- Use the flowers as part of a unit on plants and how they grow.
- Create a pattern with the placement of the flowers. Have the children try to discover what your pattern is. Let them try to discover variations of the pattern you have shown.

                   Seasonal Bulletin Boards

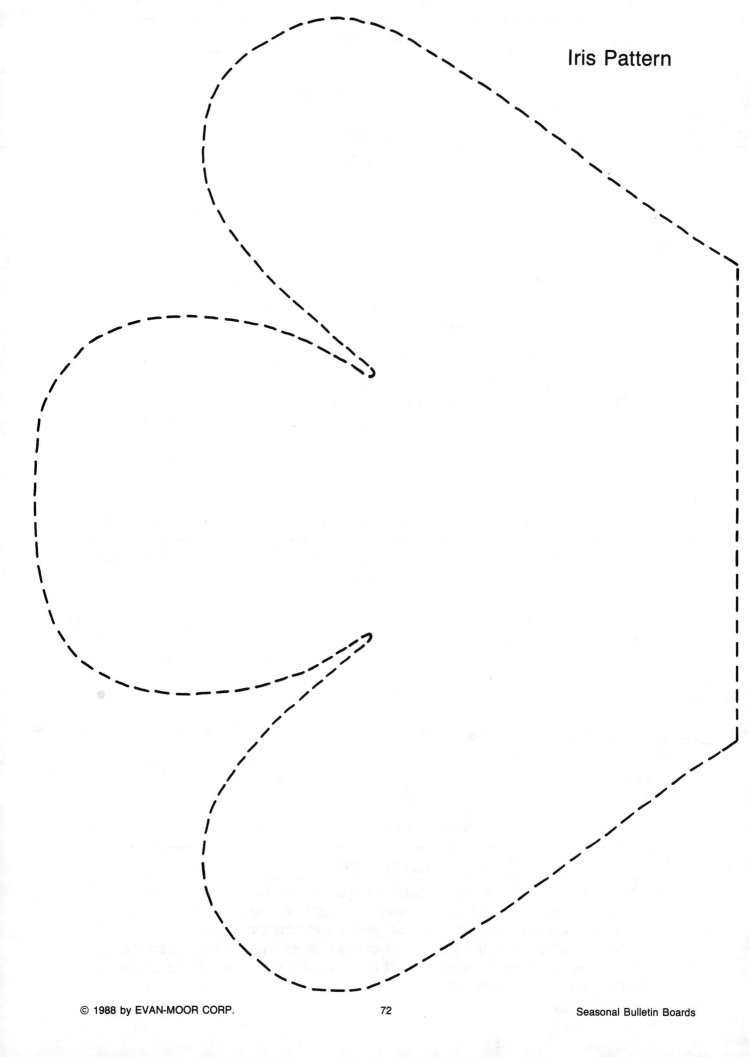

Iris Pattern

Calla Lily Pattern

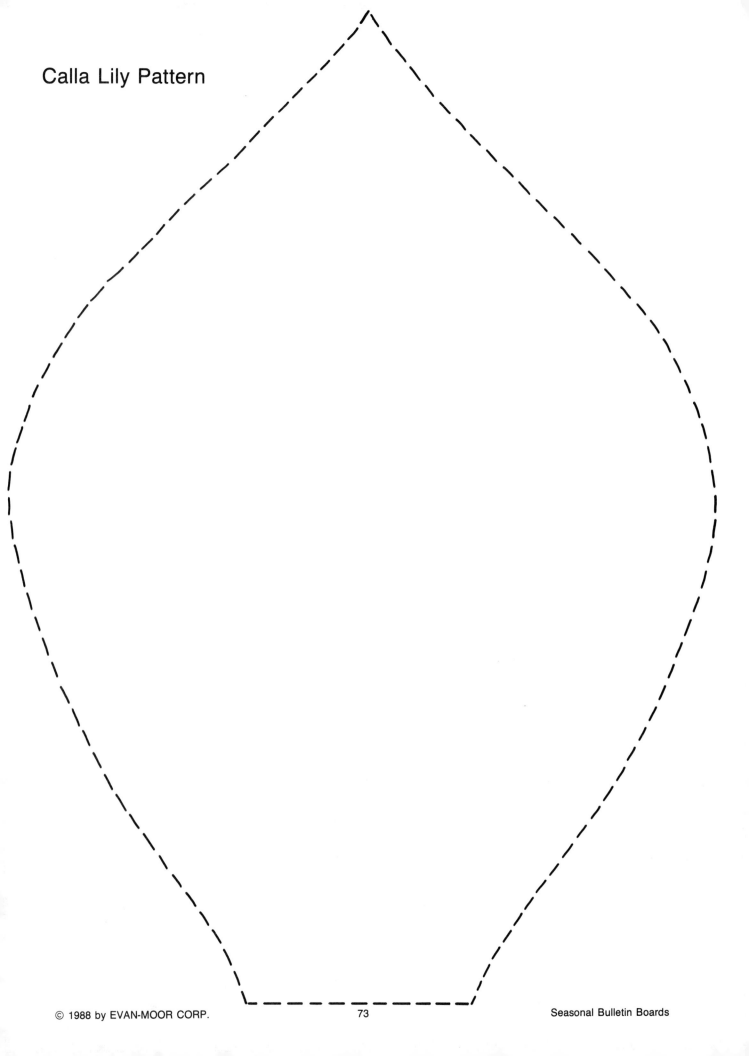

Seasonal Bulletin Boards

Daffodil Pattern

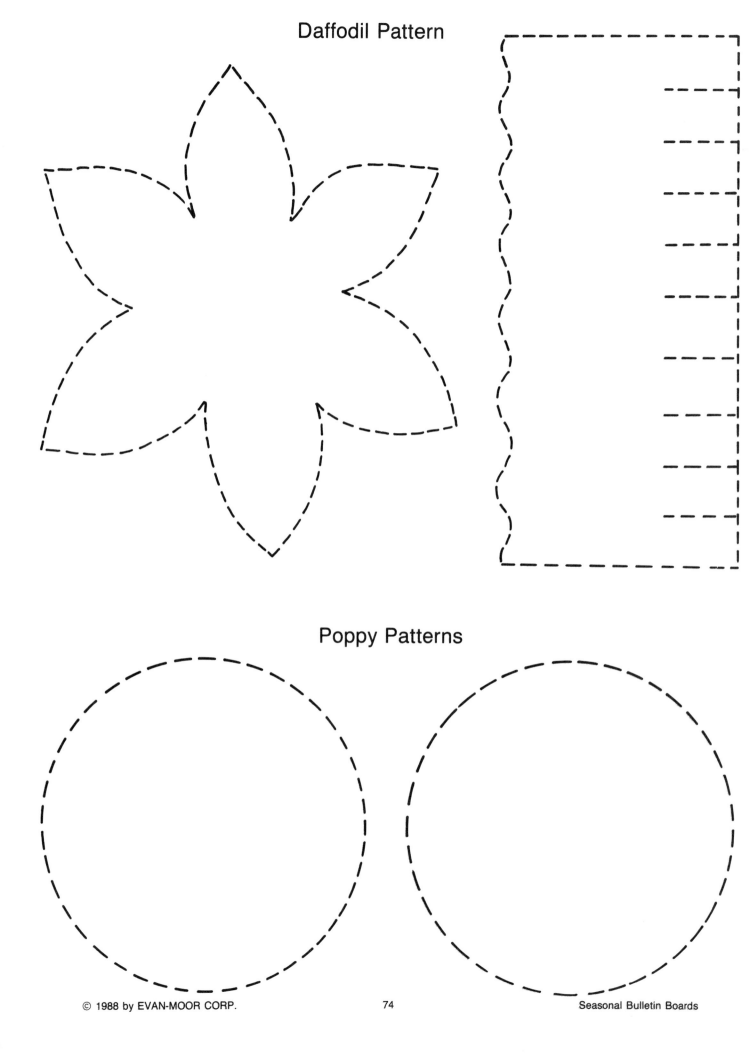

Poppy Patterns

 Seasonal Bulletin Boards

June

A board that changes...

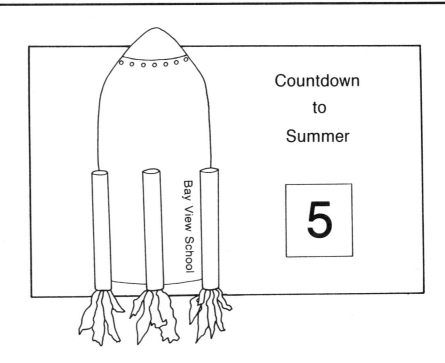

Countdown to Summer

5

Bay View School

An activity board...

June is popping out all over.

Over the chalkboard...

I am going to Grandmother's house.
In my trunk, I packed a...

Countdown to Summer

10

Background

Cover the bulletin board with blue butcher paper.

Rocket

Make a large rocket shape from butcher paper.

Fold   Cut

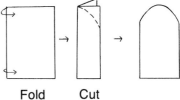

Make 3 tubes from construction paper and attach with pins to the rocket.

Add details with felt pen.

On the fifth day, tape strips of red, orange, and yellow tissue paper to the ends of the tubes. Crinkle them together and pin to the bulletin board. The rocket is beginning to fire its engines.

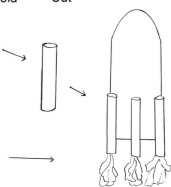

Number Cards

Cut out 11 "countdown to summer" cards from construction paper. Write one number on each card (0-10). On the back of each card, write a question about favorite remembrances of the past school year. Pin the cards in order on the bulletin board. Number 10 should be on top.

How can this bulletin board change?

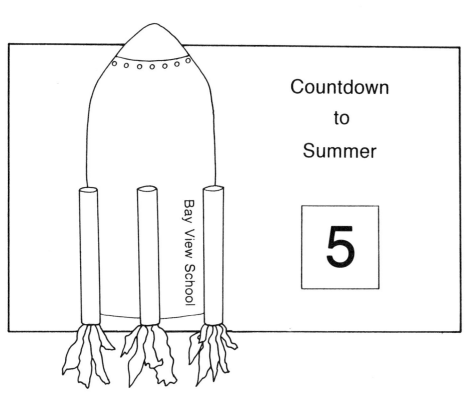

Start this countdown 10 days before school vacation starts. Remove the next card each day and read the question on the back. Discuss the question with the class.

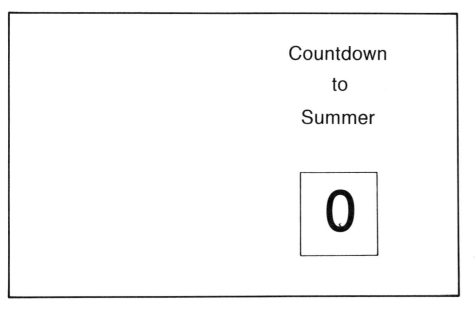

On the last day, remove the rocket and leave the board empty. Time for vacation!

Questions to use each day:

1. What art project did you enjoy the most this year?
2. What P. E. activity was the most enjoyable?
3. Was there a book you read this year that was memorable?
4. Name the writing activity you liked best.
5. What science unit was the most interesting?
6. What math concept was the most difficult this year?
7. Did you learn a favorite song this year?
8. What was the best activity at recess?
9. Could you list your favorite lunch menu?
10. What is you best memory of this school year?

 Seasonal Bulletin Boards

June is popping out all over.

Popcorn Popper

Cut the popcorn popper shape from tag.
Cover the two pieces with aluminum foil. Tape to the back of the popcorn popper to hold the foil in place.

Cut out legs and a handle from tag. Tape them to the popcorn popper.

Add a strip of yarn or roving as a cord.

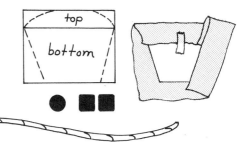

How to use:

Reproduce the popcorn kernel on page 80. Let your students copy their creative writing on the forms, and then pin them to the bulletin board.

This board is perfect for motivating creative writing. Here are some possible writing assignments:

- Write couplets.

   Write about popcorn; or help your students develop lists of rhymes about June, summer vacation activities, or favorite memories of the past school year. Use these to create a couplet or series of couplets.

- Write cinquains.

   Use this 5-line form with your class.

   > Line 1 — one word (names subject)
   > Line 2 — two words (describes subject)
   > Line 3 — three words (describes an action)
   > Line 4 — four words (expresses a feeling)
   > Line 5 — one word (refers back to line 1)

- Write descriptive paragraphs about popcorn. Include all the senses — taste, smell, sound, etc.
- Write paragraphs that describe plans for the summer or remembrances of the school year.

Over the chalkboard...

I am going to Grandmother's house.
In my trunk, I packed a...

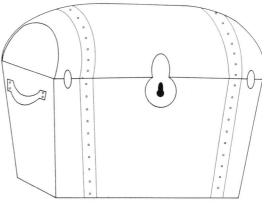

How to make:

Lay out a strip of white shelf paper as long as three-fourths of your bulletin board. Use a primary paint brush and tempera paint to letter the caption. Pencil in guide lines lightly using a yardstick.

Enlarge the trunk pattern on page 81. Use the pattern to help you draw the trunk on a large brown grocery bag. Outline it with black felt pen.

How to use:

Use spare moments before recess or lunch to play "I am going to Grandmother's house and I packed _____ in my trunk." It is a fun way to strengthen listening skills. Each time you play, select a different version of the game.

- Categories — Everything you pack in the trunk must be:
  - made of wood
  - living
  - something to wear
  - a country
- Pack for a specific kind of trip:
  - camping trip
  - trip to a big city
  - trip to the North Pole
  - trip to a foreign country
- Alphabetical order — Everything you pack must be Named in alphabetical order (a — astronaut, b — basket, etc.).

Popcorn Patterns

Trunk Pattern

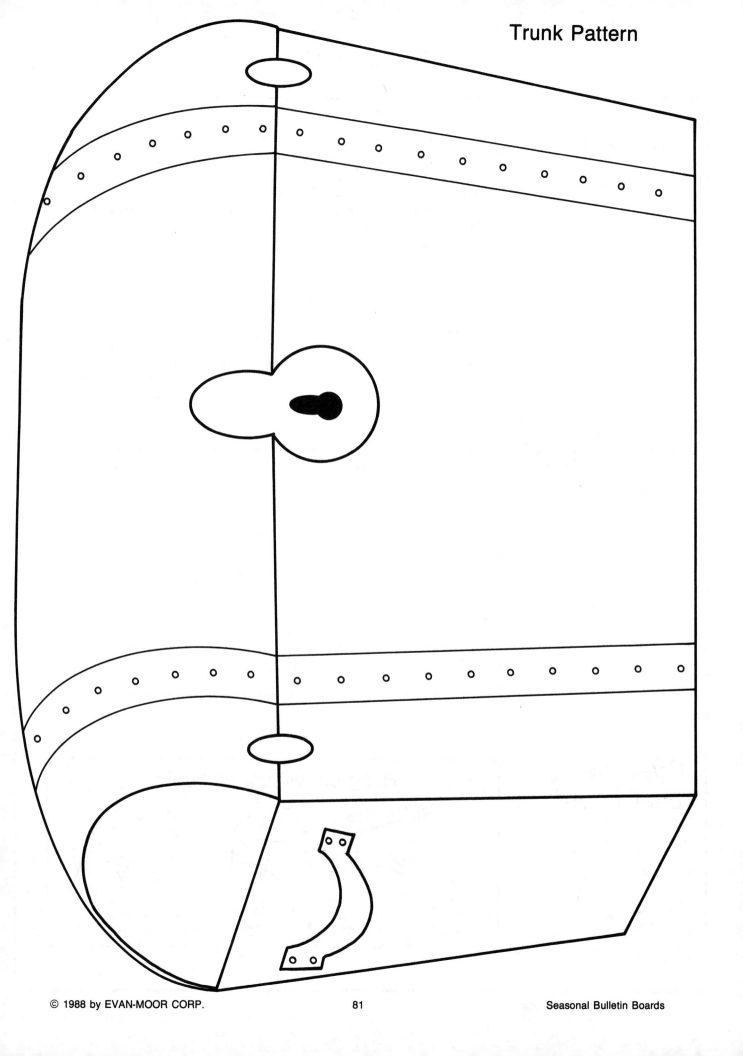

 Seasonal Bulletin Boards

Summer

An activity board...

School's out! School's out!

A board that changes...

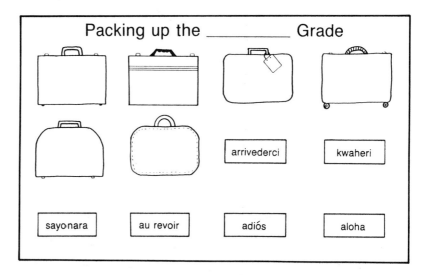

Packing up the _____ Grade

arrivederci

kwaheri

sayonara

au revoir

adiós

aloha

Over the chalkboard...

Hang out with good books!

How to make:

Background

Cover the bulletin board with blue paper.

Cut out a large yellow sun.

Cut waves from blue tissue paper.

People

1. Discuss summer plans and types of summer fun. Have the students write stories summarizing their summer plans.
2. Reproduce the patterns on page 87 and 88 for each student.
3. Paste the story paper between the head and the feet.

Students color the pictures and add details.

4. Pin the finished stories on the bulletin board.

                   Seasonal Bulletin Boards

Packing up the _____ Grade

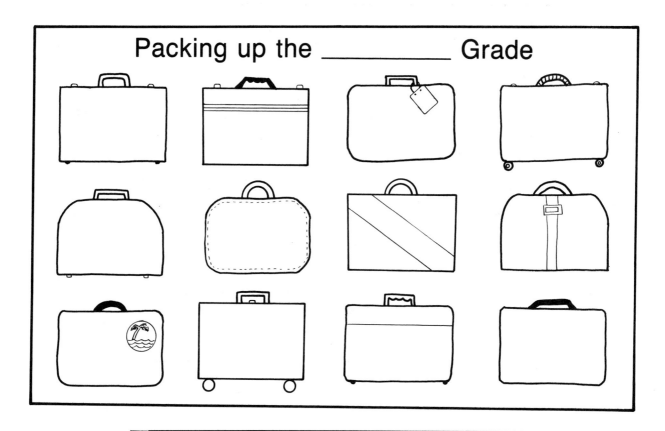

How to make:

Background

Cover the bulletin board with a brightly colored butcher paper.

Suitcases

Have children write about their favorite memories of the school year. (You'll get better results if you take time for a brainstorming session before they write.) Have each student place the finished story in a brown construction paper folder.

Round the edges on the brown folder so it looks like a suitcase.

Add a handle made from black construction paper and details with a black felt pen.

Attach a tag with the student's name.

Pin the "suitcases" to the bulletin board.

How can this bulletin board change?

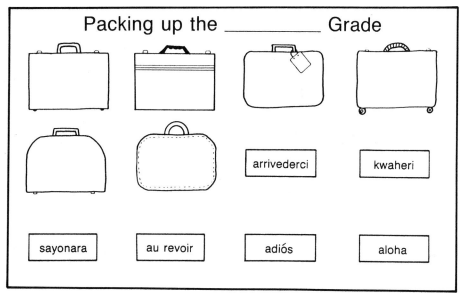

Display entire class set of suitcases and read different stories each day. Remove the suitcase after reading the story so that the board will be empty by the last day of school.

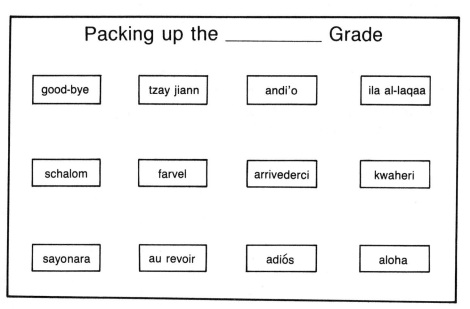

As an added surprise, under each suitcase hide a tag strip that says "good-bye" in a foreign language. Leave the strips on the board so that on the last day of school you will have a board full of "good-byes."

au revoir (French)	andi'o (Greek)	farvel (Danish)
auf Wiedersehen (German)	ila al-laqaa (Arabic)	do widzenia (Polish)
arrivederci (Italian)	schalom (Hebrew)	sbohem (Czech)
adeus (Portuguese)	seid gezund (Yiddish)	farvel (Norwegian)
do zvidániya (Russian)	sayonara (Japanese)	zbogom (Serbo-Croatian)
adiós (Spanish)	kwaheri (Swahili)	istenhozzád (Hungarian)
adio (Rumanian)	tzay jiann (Chinese)	hyvästi (Finnish)
dag (Dutch)	aloha (Hawaiian)	allaha ismarladik (Turkish)
adjö (Swedish)	good-bye (English)	selemat tinggal (Indonesian)

Over the chalkboard...

Hang out with good books!

How to make:

This board is easy to take down the last day of school. Stretch a line of rope across your board.

Have your students think seriously about their favorite author and story. Ask them to choose the *best* book they can think of to recommend to a friend. Reproduce the form on the inside back cover. Allow students time to fill in the blanks and to decorate the cover appropriately.

Hang the mock book covers from the rope with clothespins.

Other uses:
- Hang mock book covers with titles to use for creative writing.
- Hang book riddles:

    She wore a red cap and visited her grandmother.

    She took a bite from a poisoned apple.

    He tricked the wolf by going to the orchard one hour earlier.

Pattern for School's Out!

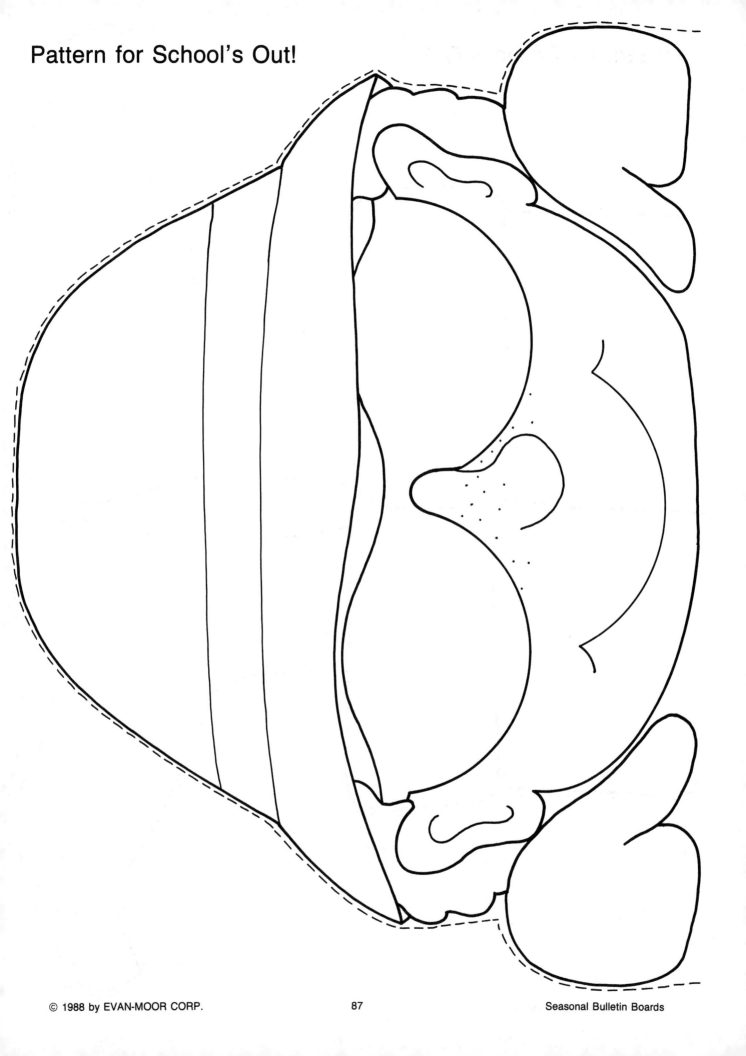

Seasonal Bulletin Boards

Pattern for School's Out!

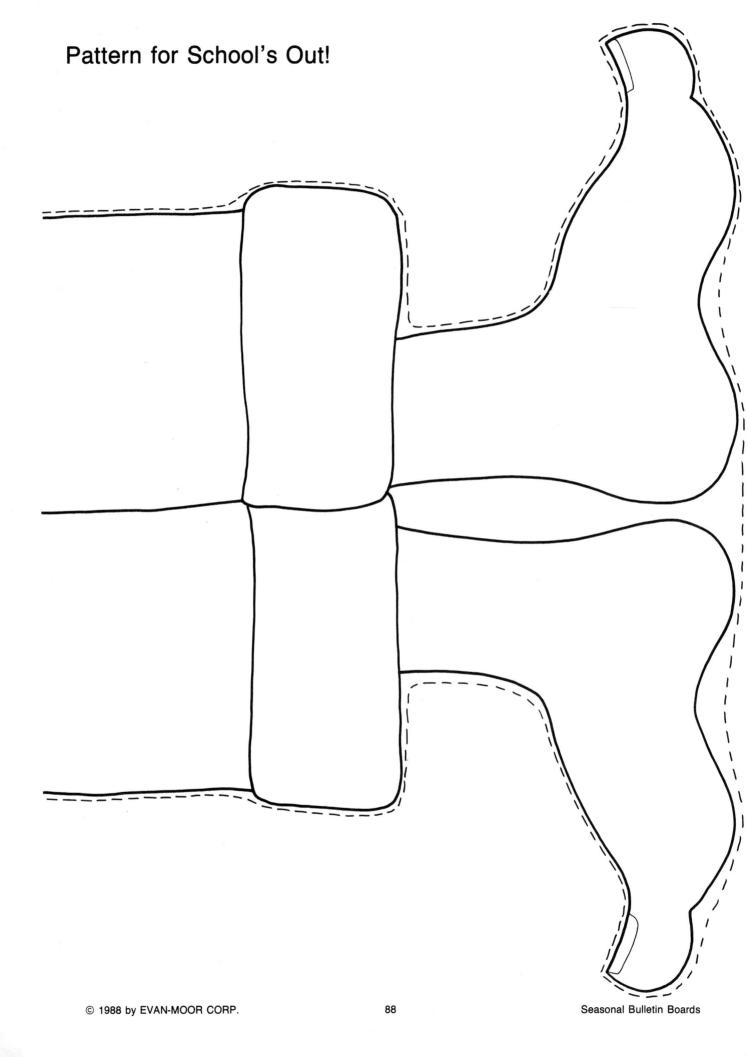

88